Alfred George Marten

Acts of Parliament and Bench Table Orders of the Inner Temple

Alfred George Marten

Acts of Parliament and Bench Table Orders of the Inner Temple

ISBN/EAN: 9783337153663

Printed in Europe, USA, Canada, Australia, Japan

Cover: Foto ©ninafisch / pixelio.de

More available books at **www.hansebooks.com**

ACTS OF PARLIAMENT

AND

BENCH TABLE ORDERS

OF

THE INNER TEMPLE.

Ordered to be printed 3 November, 1893.

ALFRED GEORGE MARTEN, ESQ., Q.C.,
TREASURER.

LONDON:
PRINTED BY H. S. CARTWRIGHT,
19, SOUTHAMPTON BUILDINGS, W.C.

1893.

CONTENTS.

I.—PRECEDENCE.
    1. Treasurer.
    2. Masters of the Bench.
    3. Junior not to be superseded.

II.—CALLS TO THE BENCH.
    4. Constitution of Bench.
    5. Qualification for Call.
    6. Disqualification for Call.
    7. Lords of Appeal and Judges. Time for calling to Bench.
    8. Honorary Benchers, &c.
    9. Only one Call a Term.
    10. How Call to be made.
    11. Proceedings on Call to Bench.
    12. Notice of Call.
    13. How Call determined.
    14. Order of Ballot.
    15. Number of votes for Call.
    16. One Ballot only.
    17. Payment of Fee and Dues.
    18. Effect of declining Call.
    19. Patent.
    20. Pensions and Preacher's Dues.

III.—TREASURER.

21. Annual Offices.
22. Readers liable.
23. Seniority decides.
24. Death or removal of Treasurer.
25. Remuneration of Treasurer.
26. Qualification.
27. Order of Succession.
28. Keeping Terms.
29. Bencher declining.
30. Books.
31. No casting vote.
32. Contracts.
33. Current Expenditure.
34. Special Expenditure.
35. Authority of Bench.
36. Cheques.
37. To ascertain the incoming Treasurer.
38. Lending Hall.
39. Power to invite guests.
40. Decision in Difficulties.
41. Ex-Treasurer.

IV.—READER.

42. Order of Succession.
43. On all Committees.
44. Coat of Arms.

V.—MASTER OF THE LIBRARY.

45. Election and Powers.
46. Library Rules.

VI.—MASTERS OF THE BENCH.
    47. Key of Library.
    48. Key of Garden.

VII.—BENCH CHAMBERS.
    49. Choice by Treasurer.
    50. Choice by Benchers.
    51. Notice of Orders.
    52. Time of disposal.
    53. Fee for admittance.
    54. No priority to Q.C.
    55. Bencher in arrear.
    56. Repairs.
    57. Accounts for repairs.
    58. Chambers dilapidated.
    59. Notice of increase of Bench Chambers.
    60. Disqualification for Chambers.
    61. Loss of Bench Chambers.

VIII.—PARLIAMENTS.
    62. Quorum.
    63. Time of holding.
    64. Adjournment.

IX.—BUSINESS AT THE BENCH TABLE.
    65. Commencement of Business.
    66. Grand Week.
    67. Minute Book.
    68. Reading Minutes.
    69. Forms of motion.
    70. Reversing decisions.
    71. Notice as to departure from Orders.
    72. Reading over Acts of Parliament.
    73. Report by F. and D. M. Committee.

X.—MONEY VOTES, APPOINTMENTS AND PENSIONS.
    74. Money Votes.
    75. Appointments, Salaries and Pensions.
    76. No right to Pension.
    77. List of Pensioners.
    78. Officers.
    79. Entry in books.
    80. Notice.
XI.—RENTING CHAMBERS.
    81. Chamber Committee.
    82. Mode of letting.
    83. Effect of ceasing to occupy.
    84. Precedence in choice.
    85. Letting to persons not Members.
    86. Second set of Chambers.
    87. No alteration without leave.
    88. Collector of Rents.
XII.—CALLING TO THE BAR.
    89. Declaration.
    90. Form of Declarations.
    91. Certificate of Sub-Treasurer.
    92. Production of Certificates.
    93. Master to vouch for character.
    94. Order to be screened.
    95. Call at Parliament after proposal.
    96. Member proposing.
    97. *Ad eundem.*
    98. Proposal day.
    99. Call Day.
    100. Notice of departure from mode.
    101. Persons in trade.

XII.—CALLING TO THE BAR (*continued*).
    102. Eminent Colonial Barristers.
    103. Voluntary compounding.
    134. Compulsory compounding.

XIII.—DISBARRING AND WITHDRAWING.
    105. Conviction of Barrister.
    106. Becoming Solicitor.
    107. Withdrawing.

XIV.—STUDENTS.
    108. Deposit on Admission.
    109. Commons Deposit.
    110. Students compounding.
    111. Who may be admitted as Students.
    112. Privilege of Solicitors.
    113. Preliminary Examination.
    114. Copy of Rules.
    115. Admission gratis.
    116. Student in arrear.

XV.—RE-ADMISSION OF STUDENTS.
    117. Conditions of re-admission.
    118. Former terms and standing allowed.

XVI.—COMMONS AND DUES.
    119. Duration.
    120. Parliament Chamber not to be used.
    121. Benchers' charge for dinner.
    122. Dinners out of Term.
    123. Barristers' charge.
    124. Students' charge.
    125. Vacations, &c., abolished.

XVI.—COMMONS AND DUES (*continued*).
    126. Students leaving Hall.
    127. Newspapers in Hall.
    128. Gowns.
    129. Not more than twenty Terms to be kept.
    130. Table of Fees.
    131. Entry of names.
    132. Accounts.
    133. Pensions and Preacher's duties.
    134. Arrears.

XVII.—CHURCH.
    135. Afternoon Preacher.
    136. Appointment.
    137. Preacher not appearing.
    138. Preacher's Deputy.
    139. Church Orders.
    140. Introducing ladies.
    141. Monuments.
    142. Expenditure on Church.
    143. No money to Church Servants.
    144. No fee for admission.

XVIII.—SUB-TREASURER.
    145. Forms.
    146. Index.
    147. Bonds.
    148. Control of Servants.
    149. Misconduct by Servants.
    150. Book of Commons.
    151. Attendance of Sub-Treasurer.
    152. Members' Names taken down.
    153. Communication to Papers.

XIX.—HOUSE.
    154. Inventories.
    155. Newspapers in Parliament Chamber.
    156. Notice as to papers to be screened.
    157. Clean linen.
    158. Waiters.
XX.—ACCOUNTS.
    159. Repairs to be separately entered.
    160. Sale of Stock.
XXI.—SURVEYOR.
    161. Orders for Work.
    162. Instructions to Workmen.
    163. Authority for Structural Alteration.
XXII.—GENERAL.
    164. Saving Order.

ACTS OF PARLIAMENT
AND
BENCH TABLE ORDERS.

PRECEDENCE.

T. O., 5 May, 1868.

1. THE Treasurer shall on all occasions have precedence of all other Masters of the Bench. — Treasurer.

2. After the Treasurer all other Masters of the Bench shall on all occasions have precedence according to the date of their Call to the Bench. — Masters of the Bench.

T. O., 23 January, 1866.

3. If a junior Bencher occupy the Treasurer's seat at dinner in the Hall, he shall afterwards occupy it in the Inner room in preference to a senior Bencher. — A Junior not to be superseded.

CALLS TO THE BENCH.

T. O., 18 *November*, 1892.
AMENDED 13 NOV. 1906.

Constitution of Bench.

4. The Bench shall consist of such Members of the Society for the time being of the Outer or Inner Bar not exceeding sixty in number as shall have been called to the Bench, and, in addition, of such Members of the Society as for the time being shall be or shall have been *SPEAKERS OF THE HOUSE OF COMMONS* Lords of Appeal, or Judges of the Supreme Court, and shall have been called to the Bench either before or after their appointments as *SPEAKERS OF THE HOUSE OF COMMONS* Lords of Appeal, or Judges.

Qualification for Call.

5. No Member of the Society of the Outer or Inner Bar shall be eligible for Call to the Bench until he shall have been called to the Bar for the space of ten years, or shall for the space of ten years have practised as a Special Pleader under the Certificates of the Bench, or shall for the space of ten years have practised

partly as a Special Pleader under such Certificates and partly as a Barrister.

6. No member of the Society shall be eligible for Call to the Bench who, for the space of ten years next previous to the day of a Call to the Bench, shall have neglected to attend the Commons in the Hall, and to pay the dues of the House.

<small>Disqualification for Call.</small>

T. O., 8 *May*, 1896.
AMENDED 13 Nov. 1906.

7. A Member of the Society (not being already a Bencher) who shall be appointed a SPEAKER OF THE HOUSE OF COMMONS Lord of Appeal, or Judge of the Supreme Court, may be proposed for Call to the Bench at any time after his appointment when a vacancy on the Bench shall occur; but, if elected, his Election shall not be deemed to fill up the vacancy then existing.

<small>Judges.</small>

8. Members of the Society (not being already Benchers) who are appointed Lords

<small>Honorary Benchers.</small>

of Appeal or Judges of the Supreme Court, may be elected Honorary Members of the Bench at any time after their appointment.

<small>Only one Call a Term</small> 9. No more than one Call to the Bench shall be made in one and the same Term.

<small>How Call to be made.</small> 10. Every Call to the Bench shall be first made at the Bench Table, and shall be afterwards confirmed in Parliament.

T. O., 9 *March,* 1900.

<small>Vacancy to be announced.</small> 11. When any vacancy occurs among the Benchers it shall be the duty of the Treasurer to announce such vacancy at the Bench Table on the first business day of the next term, and thereupon the Sub-Treasurer shall, on the following day, send notice in writing to every Bencher of the existence of such vacancy or vacancies.

12. Any Bencher may propose (or second) for Election, to fill such vacancy or vacancies, if more than one has been announced, any members of the Inn duly qualified. Every such proposal shall be in writing signed by the Proposer and Seconder, and shall be transmitted to the Treasurer, so as to be received at the Office not later than 4 p.m. on the sixth day after the Treasurer's announcement at the Bench Table. *Proposals.*

13*a*. The Treasurer shall cause to be prepared a list of all the proposals received by him with, in the case of each Candidate, the date of his call to the Bar, and, if a Queen's Counsel, the date of his taking silk, his professional address, description and circuit, if any, and the name of his proposer, and seconder; such list shall be laid before the Bench at the Bench Table next after the last day for sending in proposals. *List of Candidates.*

Date of Election.	13*b*. When such list is presented, the Bench shall fix the day of Election, being a day not less than six nor more than fourteen days after the presentation of such list.
Notice.	13*c*. A copy of such list, with notice of the day fixed for the Election, shall forthwith be sent to each Bencher, and shall be laid upon the table in the Benchers' room.
Elections on the same day.	13*d*. When there are more vacancies than one to be filled the Elections shall all be held on the same day.
Not more Candidates than Vacancies.	14. When there are not more Candidates than there are vacancies the name or names of the Candidate or Candidates shall at once be submitted, in the order of their precedence at the Bar, for election by ballot and Call to the Bench.
More Candidates than Vacancies.	14*a*. When there are more Candidates than vacancies—

(1) The Selection of a Candidate to be submitted for ballot to fill each vacancy shall be taken separately. — Selections separately.

(2) The Selection shall be by voting papers. — Voting Papers.

(3) On the day of Election each Bencher present shall be supplied with a voting paper containing the list of Candidates. — For each Bencher.

(4) If he wishes to vote he shall put a mark against the name of that Candidate only for whom he wishes to vote to fill the vacancy in respect of which the votes are being taken. — One mark only.

(5) Two Scrutineers shall be appointed by the Bench; they shall collect the voting papers, and shall allot to each Candidate the votes given in his favour. — Scrutineers.

Candidate with absolute Majority.	(6) If, on the first voting, any Candidate shall have obtained an absolute majority of the votes given, his name shall thereupon be submitted for election by ballot.
No absolute Majority.	(7) If, on the first voting, no Candidate shall have obtained such an absolute majority, the name of the Candidate who has obtained the smallest number of votes, and the name or names of any other Candidate or Candidates who may not have obtained one-fourth of the votes, shall be struck out and a fresh vote shall be taken on the remaining names. If necessary, this shall be repeated till some Candidate has obtained such an absolute majority; his name shall thereupon be submitted for election by ballot.

(8) If, on any voting, two names only are sent round, and the two Candidates receive an equal number of votes, the name of the senior in precedence at the Bar shall be submitted for election by ballot. *Equal number of Votes.*

(9) If, on any other voting, the two or more Candidates who have obtained the smallest number of votes shall have obtained an equal number, being at least one-fourth, of the votes given, the name of the junior in precedence at the Bar shall be struck out. *Senior to be selected.*

15. The ballot box shall not go round more than once with respect to any Candidate. *One ballot only.*

16. In order to the Call of any member of the Society to the Bench there must be not *Number of Votes for Call*

less than twenty Benchers present at the Bench Table, and there must be not less than twenty Benchers voting by ballot in the Candidate's favour.

<small>Votes against.</small> 16*a*. Should there be four or more Benchers voting against any Candidate he shall be declared not to have been elected.

<small>Candidate not elected.</small> 16*b*. Any Candidate who, after his name has been submitted for election by ballot, has been declared not to have been elected by reason of four or more Benchers having voted against him, shall not be eligible again until after the expiration of the three next terms.

<small>Vacancy not filled.</small> 16*c*. If a Candidate, whose name has been submitted for election by ballot, shall be declared not to have been elected the vacancy for which that ballot was taken shall not be filled till the next term, and shall then be

announced and dealt with in all respects as if it were a new vacancy.

T. O., 24 January, 1899.

17. Every Member of the Society called to the Bench shall, before his Call is confirmed in Parliament, pay to the Society the fee of £210, and all commons and dues then owing by him to the Society.   *Payment of Fee and Dues.*

17a. On any future Election to the Bench the right to Bench Chambers of the person elected shall be abolished.   *Abolition of Bench Chambers.*

18. Any Member of the Society who shall be called to the Bench and shall decline the invitation, shall not be afterwards proposed for Call to the Bench.   *Effect of declining Call.*

T. O., 4 July, 1851.

19. When a Patent of Queen's Counsel or Precedence is sent in to the Treasurer, it is to be forthwith returned with an intimation   *Patent.*

that it has been duly entered on the books of the Society.

T. O., 13 *June*, 1884.

Pensions and Preacher's Dues.

20. No Pensions or Preacher's dues are due from any Bencher between the time of his election to the Bench and his obtaining a Bench Chamber.

TREASURER.

A. P., 29 *June*, 1691.

T. O., 1 *Feb.*, 1828.

Annual Office.

21. WHEREAS it hath been found by experience of this Society, and other Societies of the Law, that the yearly constituting of a new Treasurer in the Term of St. Michael doth much conduce to the ascertaining the revenue and other benefits of the Society.

Be it therefore enacted that no Treasurer of this Society shall continue in the office of Treasurer longer than for the space of one whole year, and that a new Treasurer shall be every year constituted and made at the second Parliament in Michaelmas Term; but in order to obviate the inconveniences which have been found to arise from the circumstance of the Treasurer's official duties commencing on the day of his election, the retiring Treasurer shall continue in office until the last day of December (inclusive) retaining the privileges and discharging the duties in the same manner as during the former part of his Treasurership.

A. P., 29 *June*, 1691.

22. The said office of Treasurer shall be executed by all the Benchers of this Society that have been or are liable to be Readers successively, and in their turn according to their respective seniority at the Bench.

Readers liable.

A. P., 29 *June*, 1691.

„ 8 *February*, 1771.

Seniority decides.

23. No Counsel of their present Majesties or their successors or any other person whatsoever shall hereafter be made Treasurer but according to their seniority in time at the Bench of this Society.

Death or removal of Treasurer.

24. In case of the death or removal of a Treasurer in his year, the next Bencher capable as aforesaid shall be constituted Treasurer at the next Parliament held for the said Society, which Treasurer shall hold the same for the remaining part of the said year, instead of the said Treasurer so dead or removed, and be continued for the year next ensuing at the second Parliament in Michaelmas Term.

Remuneration of Treasurer.

25. And for the encouragement of the Treasurer of this Society in the careful attending and executing the said office, forasmuch that

every Treasurer of this Society is by virtue of the said office obliged to give his constant attendance upon the service of the House during the whole Terms, for perusing the several Acts and Orders of this House before they are entered, and in receiving and taking the several accounts of all sums of money received and paid out for the use of the said Society, and for divers other matters relating to the said office (as is hereby declared he ought to do):

Be it therefore enacted that the present Treasurer, and every other Treasurer hereafter so to be yearly constituted and made as aforesaid, shall be allowed upon his account the sum of £100, and so proportionately for the time of his service in the said office, and that no Treasurer shall claim any further or other recompense or allowance for or by reason of his service in the said office.

26. No Bencher of this Society shall be   Qualification.

capable of the said office of Treasurer until he hath been at the Bench for the space of three years at the least, except the Attorney and Solicitor-General.

<small>Order of Succession.</small>

27. No Bencher of this Society whatsoever shall be constituted and made Treasurer a second time, until all other the Benchers who are or shall be capable thereof shall have first held and served in the said office, except in the case of death or removal as aforesaid.

A. P., 10 *November*, 1697.

<small>Keeping Terms.</small>

28. No Bencher of this Society shall hereafter be capable of being chosen Treasurer of this Society unless he shall have kept the two precedent Terms before such election, and shall have been personally present at the Bench Table four times at the least in each of the said Terms, except upon such reasonable excuse

offered for his absence as shall be allowed by the Table in each of the said precedent Terms.

A. P., 21 *November*, 1746.

29. If any Bencher hath declined or shall once decline being Treasurer, or hath been or shall be set aside as not qualified for that office by the Rules and Orders of this Society, and another Bencher be chosen in his stead, such person so declining or set aside shall for ever after be disqualified for, and incapable of holding, the said office. Bencher declining.

T. O., 7 *June*, 1825.

30. The Treasurer is authorised to expend £50 per annum, to be laid out in books at the discretion of the Treasurer. Books.

T. O., 12 *November*, 1878.

31. In cases of election to the Bench, or of Officers of the Society, and on all other No casting vote.

questions, the Treasurer or Master of the Bench presiding has but one vote.

T. O., 7 *May*, 1889.

Contracts.   32. All Contracts entered into on behalf of the Society shall be made in the name of the Treasurer for the time being.

Current Expenditure.   33. The Treasurer may enter into Contracts providing for the ordinary current expenditure of the Society. He shall, however, in making such Contracts act with the consent of the Finance, Wine, Library, or other Committees respectively, in accordance with the practice for the time being.

Special Expenditure.   34. The Treasurer may also expend on behalf of the Society from time to time sums of money, provided that no one sum shall exceed £50, and that all such sums in any one year shall not exceed £200.

35. Except as provided otherwise in Orders 33 and 34, the Treasurer shall have no power to enter into any Contract without the authority of the Bench. <small>Authority of Bench.</small>

36. All cheques drawn on behalf of the Society shall be signed by the Treasurer for the time being and one other Bencher, and countersigned by the Sub-Treasurer. <small>Cheques.</small>

T. O., 8 *June,* 1883.

37. The Sub-Treasurer is authorised in each succeeding Hilary Term to ask, in writing, the Reader for the time being— <small>To ascertain the incoming Treasurer.</small>

(1) Whether he wishes (if elected) to serve as Treasurer in the following year; and, if he answers in the negative, to ask him

B

(2) To send in at once, to the Treasurer's Office, his written resignation of the Readership, which office will then *ipso facto* pass to the Bencher next in seniority.

The Sub-Treasurer shall, with all convenient speed, put the same questions (if necesssary) to each successive Reader until he reaches one who expresses his wish, or who does not refuse (if elected) to serve as Treasurer.

The Sub-Treasurer is to do his utmost to conclude this enquiry before the 1st day of Easter Term, and the Treasurer is to report to the Bench, not later than the second business day in Easter Term, the name of the Bencher who has accepted the office of Reader, with a view (if elected) of serving as Treasurer during the following year.

T. O., 23 *June,* 1843.

Lending Hall. 38. Neither the Treasurer nor any Master of

the Bench has any right to lend the use of the Hall or any part of the premises belonging to the House for any purpose not connected with the Society without the consent of the Bench Table.

T. O., 25 January, 1881.

39. The Treasurer shall use his discretion as to the number of guests he shall think fit to invite on behalf of the Inn to dine at the Bench Table on the Grand Day of each Term. *Power to invite guests.*

T. O., 16 April, 1858.

40. In all cases of difficulty or dispute in carrying into effect these Rules, the decision of the Treasurer or Chairman for the time being shall be final. *Decision in difficulties.*

T. O., 22 November, 1870.

41. The ex-Treasurer shall be placed on all Committees for the year. *Ex-Treasurer*

READER.

T. O., 16 *May*, 1702.

Order of Succession.

42. EACH Master of the Bench in succession is chosen Reader without option on his part, after which his Coat of Arms is emblazoned in the Hall. The following year (if otherwise duly qualified) he is eligible to be elected Treasurer.

T. O., 22 *November*, 1870.

On all Committees.

43. The Reader for the year shall be placed on all Committees for that year.

T. O., 25 *November*, 1670.

Coat of Arms.

44. Committee to treat with a Herald Painter for setting up all the Readers' Coats of Arms.

MASTER OF THE LIBRARY.

T. O., 7 *June*, 1825.

Election and Powers.

45. ONE of the Masters of the Bench shall be annually elected Master of the Library and be placed on the Library Committee for the year, and be authorised to expend Fifty

Pounds in the purchase of Books for the Library, in addition to the Fifty Pounds at the disposal of the Treasurer.

The election of the Master of the Library shall be on the same day as that of the Treasurer in Michaelmas Term.

T. O., 21 *June*, 1825.

46. The Rules regulating the Library are printed and hung up in the Library. Library Rules.

MASTERS OF THE BENCH.

T. O., 9 *February*, 1709.

47. EVERY Bencher on his Call receives a key of the Library, and possesses the privilege of taking out for perusal any number of volumes, on entering their titles in a book kept for the purpose in the Reading Room. Key of Library.

The Library key gives access also to the Hall and Parliament Chambers.

T. O., 5 June, 1888.

Key of Garden

48. Every Master of the Bench has for his own use a key which opens the Garden Gates, and the power of granting written orders of admission from 8 a.m. till dusk; but the power of granting keys of the Garden is vested in the Master of the Garden alone, and shall only be exercised by him in favour of persons occupying chambers in the Inn, not Masters of the Bench. Any such person receiving a key shall deposit with the Sub-Treasurer the sum of £1 1s., to be retained by him till the key is returned by the person to whom it was issued.

BENCH CHAMBERS

A. P., 9 *February,* 1776.

Choice by Treasurer.

49. For the future the Treasurer shall be entitled to the choice of all Bench Chambers that may fall to the House during his Treasurership to the day that the new Treasurer enters on his office whenever the same are disposed of.

A. P., 19 *November*, 1691.
„ 14 *June*, 1771.
T. O., 22 *May*, 1821.
„ 5 *June*, 1883.
„ 20 *November*, 1883.

50. Whereas, by the usage and custom of this Society, the choice of Chambers by the Masters of the Bench hath always been and ought to be according to their seniority and priority of sitting at the Bench Table, subject to the choice of the Treasurer: And whereas it hath been observed that some Masters of the Bench do, from Term to Term, absent themselves from the Bench Table, and do not give their due assistance in the debating and ordering the affairs of the House and upholding the exercise thereof,—and yet nevertheless will come and be present at Parliaments held for this Society, and expect to vote and have their choice and election of Chambers there accord-

Choice by Benchers.

ing to such their seniority, equally with those that are frequent in Commons, and do duly attend the business and exercise of the House; by reason and means whereof the business of the House hath been often neglected and the exercise failed, to the great prejudice and dishonour of this Society: Be it therefore enacted, that from henceforth no Bencher of this Society shall have a vote or election of a Chamber of any Parliament hereafter to be holden for this Society, unless he shall have been personally present at the Bench Table and in Commons four several days, at the least, in each of the two precedent Terms before such Parliament [except upon such reasonable excuse offered for his absence as shall be allowed by the Table], any law, usage or custom to the contrary notwithstanding.

T. O., 30 *June*, 1797.

Notice of Orders.

51 In future so much of the copies of the

Orders of the 19th November, 1691 (*par.* 50), and 10th November, 1697 (*par.* 28), as relates to the manner of keeping Commons to qualify for a Bench Chamber and for the office of Treasurer, be delivered to such gentlemen as shall hereafter be called to the Bench of this Society.

A. P., 15 *June*, 1686.
„ 20 *November*, 1730.

52. When a Bench Chamber devolves to the House, it is disposed of on the last Parliament Day in the next, or present Term, notice to be given to the Bench Table four days previously. {Time of disposal.}

53. Each Master of the Bench on accepting or exchanging a Bench Chamber pays £2 (for admittance) to the Society. {Fee for admittance.}

A. P., 6 *February*, 1714.

No priority to Q.C.
54. No priority is given to Queen's Counsel in the choice of Bench Chambers.

T. O., 12 *June*, 1708.

Bencher in arrear.
55. Any Bencher who shall owe more than £10 for Commons (three days after demand) is incapacitated from choosing a Bench Chamber, as well as from voting at the Table or Parliament.

T. O., 24 *November*, 1773.

Repairs.
56. No ornamental repairs to be done to any Bench Chambers at the expense of the House, but such repairs only shall be done at the expense of the Society as are necessary for the supporting and maintaining the buildings.

T. O., 9 *November*, 1710.

Accounts for repairs.
57. Sub-Treasurer for the future to pay all allowances for repairs of Bench Chambers, and to be allowed it in his accounts.

T. O., 21 *December*, 1759.

58. When the Bench Chambers of any Bencher are in a dilapidated condition, a Committee is appointed to allot Chambers of equal value in lieu thereof.

<small>Chambers dilapidated.</small>

T. O., 6 *May*, 1743.

59. When a motion made for increasing Bench Chambers, the same not to be taken into consideration in the same Term it was made, but the same shall be adjourned until the next Term upon notice to be given in writing by the Sub-Treasurer 10 days at least to every Master of the Bench before the same is appointed to come on and not otherwise.

<small>Notice of increase of Bench Chambers.</small>

T. O., 7 *February*, 1758.

60. No Bencher of this Society who shall accept of a Call to the Bench in any other Society shall from thenceforth be entitled to

<small>Disqualification for Chambers.</small>

the choice of or be capable of being admitted to any Bench Chamber within this Society, or shall be capable of being elected or appointed Treasurer of this Society.

<small>Loss of Bench Chambers.</small>

61. If any Bencher of this House, after his admission to Bench Chambers in this Society, or during the time he shall be Treasurer of this Society, shall accept of a Call to the Bench in any other Society, then and in such case he shall no longer continue to hold or enjoy any such Bench Chamber, or the office of Treasurer of this Society, or to receive or take any benefit or advantage therefrom, but his admission to such Bench Chamber, and his appointment to the said office of Treasurer of this Society, shall from thenceforth cease and be void to all intents and purposes as fully and effectually as if the person so called to the Bench of any other Society was immediately after such Call actually deceased.

PARLIAMENTS.

62. FIVE Benchers, besides the Treasurer, constitute a Parliament.   *Quorum.*

T. O., 20 *November* 1767.

63. No Parliaments are held on any other days than Fridays in every Term except when the Call Day falls on any other day, and except by an Order of the Table made two days before such Parliament is to be holden, and a copy of such Order to be sent to the Masters of the Bench in town.   *Time of holding.*

T. O., 25 *November*, 1767.

64. The last mentioned Order not to extend to any Parliament held by adjournment, provided the Parliament adjourned was held on a Friday, or on any other day in virtue of an Order made two days before.   *Adjournment*

BUSINESS AT THE BENCH TABLE.

T. O., 23 *November*, 1827.

„ 8 *November*, 1889.

Commencement of Business.
65. Business shall commence on the first Tuesday or Friday, whichever shall first happen in every Term, and business days out of Term are held when appointed by the Treasurer; a Bench Table shall be held on the first Tuesday or Friday after October 23rd.

T. O., 13 *May*, 1728.

Grand Week.
66. Business may be proposed and done on any day in the Grand Week in any Term except the Grand Day.

T. O., 15 *May*, 1821.

Minute Book.
67. The proceedings of the Bench shall be daily entered in a rough minute book and be brought up every evening to the Parliament Chamber for the signature of the Treasurer or the senior Bencher present.

T. O., 20 *July*, 1894.

Appointment of Committees.

65*a*. All standing Committees shall be elected yearly in Michaelmas Term on a day to be named by the Treasurer, the first election to be held next Michaelmas Term (1894). Members, shall go out of office on the day before the day of election and shall be eligible for re-election. And the Treasurer in each year shall ascertain in or before Michaelmas Term what Members of Committees are willing to serve in the following year.

T. O., 12 *June*, 1857.

68. On every business day the proceedings of the preceding business day be first read over and signed. — Reading Minutes.

69. No motion can be put from the Chair unless the same is reduced into writing. — Form of motion.

T. O., 31 *May*, 1872.

70. When a subject has been discussed, and a decision arrived at by the Bench, no motion shall be made to revive discussion or reverse the decision on the same subject in the same Term. — Reversing decisions.

T. O., 21 *November*, 1732.

71. If anything shall be hereafter moved at the Bench Table contrary to any former Order, nothing shall be done thereupon, but upon a day appointed for that purpose, and notice to be given to the Masters in town at least three days before such day. — Notice as to departure from Orders.

T. O., 22 January, 1858.

Reading over Acts of Parliament.
72. The proceedings of the last Parliament shall be read at the next Bench Meeting in Term.

T. O., 29 February, 1884.

Report by F. and D. M. Committee.
73. The Finance and Domestic Management Committee report on the first business day of each Term.

MONEY VOTES, APPOINTMENTS, AND PENSIONS.

T. O., 29 April, 1845.

Money votes.
74. No vote of money shall be given out of the funds of this Society without a previous notice of fourteen days being sent round to the Masters of the Bench.

T. O., 19 January, 1883.

Appointments, Salaries, and Pensions.
75. The report of a Committee upon any appointment, salary or pension, shall be laid

upon the table in the Benchers' Room, and be considered by the Bench upon the second business day after it shall be so laid.

T. O., 11 *December,* 1873.

76. All persons who shall hereafter enter into the employment or service of the Inn shall be informed on their entering into the service that they will not be entitled to claim any pension.

No right to Pension.

T. O., 2 *February,* 1858.

77. A list of the Pensioners of the Society shall be annually submitted to the Bench in Trinity Term.

List of Pensioners.

A. P., 12 *June*, 1695.

78. For the future the office of Sub-Treasurer, Steward, Chief Butler, and Head Cook of this Society be appointed by the Bench Table, and confirmed by Act of Parliament of the same Society; all other Officers and Servants

Officers.

of this Society for the future, if they happen to fall or become void in Term time, shall be appointed by the Bench Table of the said Society. But if they happen to fall or become void in the Vacation time, the same shall be appointed, and placed in by the Treasurer for the time being.

<small>Entry in books.</small>
79. All Officers and Servants of this Society that shall be placed into any of the offices or services belonging to the same by the Treasurer or Bench Table, shall be accordingly entered in the House books belonging to the said Society.

T. O., 26 *January*, 1790.

<small>Notice.</small>
80. No appointment of an officer, servant, or tradesman, ought to be made in Term time, without reasonable notice to the Benchers in town.

RENTING CHAMBERS.

T. O., 16 *November*, 1819.

81. A STANDING Committee shall be appointed to superintend the letting of all the Chambers of this Society, whether Bench Chambers or others, with approbation of the Benchers as to their Chambers, and in future no Chambers to be let without the sanction of the Committee.

Chamber Committee.

T. O., 22 *November*, 1892.

82. Upon a set of Chambers becoming vacant the Treasurer shall send notice of the vacancy to all Members of the Inn who have previously intimated their desire to rent Chambers. On the expiration of seven days from the sending of such notice the Chambers shall, subject to the sanction of the Committee, be let to the senior Applicant, who shall bonâ fide

Mode of letting.

desire to rent them for his own personal occupation, and who shall have declared such his desire in writing. If no Member of the Inn shall declare his desire to rent the Chambers for his own personal occupation, the same may, subject to the sanction of the Committee, be let to the Senior Applicant desirous of renting the same without his making such declaration.

Effect of ceasing to occupy.

83. If any Member of the Inn to whom Chambers have been let for his own personal occupation shall cease to occupy them personally, he shall forthwith give notice thereof to the Treasurer, and in case he shall fail to give such notice the Society shall be entitled to determine his tenancy, and to require him to deliver up possession of such Chambers at any time on giving him not less than seven days' notice.

84. Subject to Rules 87 and 88, and to the decision of the Committee, the Members of the Inn not being Benchers shall have precedence in the choice for renting Chambers according to their seniority in Membership, and Queen's Counsel shall have no right to priority in choice over Members of the Outer Bar.

Precedence in choice.

85. If after the offer of any set of Chambers no Member of the Inn approved by the Committee shall desire to rent the same, the same may be let with the sanction of the Committee to any Barrister or Member of any other Inn of Court, or in default of any application for the same by any Barrister or Member of any other Inn of Court then to any other person.

Letting to persons not Members.

86. No person renting or holding one set of Chambers shall hereafter, without the special sanction of the Committee, have any other set of Chambers let to him unless he shall

Second set of Chambers.

surrender and give up possession of the set already rented or held.

T. O., 22 *May*, 1701.

No alteration without leave.
87. No alteration to be made in the Buildings or Chambers of this House without leave asked of the Bench Table.

T. O., 13 *July*, 1821.

Collector of Rents.
88. The rents of all the Chambers belonging to this Society (except those appropriated to Benchers) shall be collected by the Collector and paid by him daily as received into the Bankers of the Society, to be placed to the Rent Account of the Society, and an account of all such receipts and payments shall be kept by the Collector to be produced half-yearly to the Committee appointed for investigating the funds of the Society.

The accounts to be delivered to the Sub-Treasurer half-yearly for payment.

CALLING TO THE BAR.

T. O., 30 *November*, 1680.

89. No names of Students to be proposed for the Bar unless their full time be allowed by the House and approved by the Treasurer, and the usual declaration by a Student before his Call to the Bar has been made.

Declaration.

T. O., 4 *November*, 1892.

90. The Declaration to be made by Students upon Call to the Bar shall be in the following form :—

Form of Declarations.

PROPOSAL FOR THE BAR.

Declaration to be made by a Student before Call to the Bar.

I,

being desirous of being called to the Bar by the Honourable Society of the Inner Temple, do hereby declare and undertake as follows :—

1.—That I am not a person in Holy Orders [or, that I, being a person in Holy Orders, have not during the year next before the date of this Declaration held or performed any Clerical preferment or duty, or performed any Clerical functions, and do not intend any longer to act as a Clergyman].

2.—That I am not and have never since my Admission as a Student of this Honourable Society been an Attorney-at-Law, a Solicitor, a Writer to the Signet, a Writer of the Scotch Courts, a Proctor, a Notary Public, a Clerk in Chancery, a Parliamentary Agent, an Agent in any Court original or appellate, a Clerk to any Justice of the Peace, a Registrar of any Court, an Official Provisional Assistant or Deputy Receiver or Liquidator under any Bankruptcy or Winding-up Act, or acted directly or indirectly in any such or similar capacity, or in the capacity of Clerk of or to any of the persons above described, or in the service of any of the persons above described (*except as a Pupil in a Solicitor's Office*), or as Clerk of or to any Judge, Barrister, Conveyancer, Special Pleader, Equity Draftsman, or Clerk of the Peace, or of or to any Officer in any Court of Justice.

3.—That I will not, if Called to the Bar, and while and so long as I remain a Barrister, be or act as an Attorney-at-Law, a Solicitor, a Writer to the

Signet, a Writer of the Scotch Courts, a Proctor, a Notary Public, a Clerk in Chancery, a Parliamentary Agent, an Agent in any Court original or appellate, a Clerk to any Justice of the Peace, or act directly or indirectly in any such or similar capacity, or in the capacity of Clerk of or to any of the persons above described, or in the service of any of the persons above described, or be or act as Clerk of or to any Judge, Barrister, Conveyancer, Special Pleader, Equity Draftsman, or Clerk of the Peace, or of or to any Officer in any Court of Justice, and that I will not while and so long as I am in practice as a Barrister be or act as a Registrar of any Court, or be or act as an Official Provisional Assistant or Deputy Receiver or Liquidator under any Bankruptcy or Winding-up Act, or be or act as Clerk of or to any such Registrar, Receiver, or Liquidator, or act in any such or a similar capacity, or be or act in the service of any such Registrar, Receiver, or Liquidator.

Dated this   day of   , 189

Signature

ORDERED—That no Master of the Bench do from henceforth propose any of this Society to be called to the Degree of the Bar, without he is able to give some account to their Masterships (if required) of the character and qualifications of the gentleman he proposes. (Bench Table, 16th June, 1789.)

𝔍 intend to propose the Call to the Bar of Mr.

in   Term, 189

To
The Sub-Treasurer of   *Bencher.*
the Inner Temple
189

T. O., 21 *November*, 1762.
„   11 *June*, 1730.

Certificate of Sub-Treasurer.

91. No Master of the Bench to move to put any person into the paper for the Call to the Bar, unless upon a Certificate from the Sub-Treasurer of his standing and other qualifications.

T. O., 8 *February*, 1739.

Production of Certificates.

92. The certificates to be laid before the

Table by the Sub-Treasurer at least two days before the motion is made for the Call.

T. O., 16 *June*, 1789.

93. No Master of the Bench do from henceforth propose any Member of this Society to be called to the Degree of the Bar, without he is able to give some account to their Masterships (if required) of the character and qualifications of the gentleman he proposes.   Master to vouch for character.

T. O., 27 *November*, 1807.

94. The last mentioned Bench Table Order shall be screened in the Hall.   Order to be screened.

T. O., 16 *June*, 1789.

95. No person in this Society to be called to the Bar until the next Parliament after that at which such person shall have been proposed by one of the Masters of the Bench.   Call at Parliament after Proposal.

T. O., 27 *November*, 1807.

Member proposing.

96. The name of the Master of the Bench who proposes each gentleman to be called to be inserted in the paper containing a list of the Candidates.

T. O., 12 *June*, 1838.

Ad eundem.

97. No person be hereafter admitted *ad eundem* of this Society after his Call to the Bar.

T. O., 25 *May*, 1852.

Proposal day.

98. Tuesday in the week before the Call Day in each Term, shall be the day for proposing gentlemen for Call to the Bar.

T. O., 16 *April*, 1852.
„   21 *March*, 1884.

Call Day.

99. No Call to the Bar shall take place except during a Term; and such Call shall be made on the same day by each of the Inns,

In lieu of *T. O.* 98 which has been abolished the following is substituted :—

T. O., 8 June, 1894.

The Business Day next but one preceding the Call Day in each Term shall be the day for proposing Members of this Society for Call to the Bar.

T. O. 27 *April* 1904.

Admission *ad eundem.*

97. The Table Order of 12 June 1838 is rescinded.

A Barrister of another Inn may, by a special order of the Bench, be admitted *ad eundem* of this Society.

Six days before any such admission the name of the applicant shall be screened in the Hall and the Parliament Chamber and be sent round to every Master of the Bench.

The fee on admission *ad eundem* of this Society shall be £60.

namely, on the 16th day of each Term, unless such day shall happen to be Saturday or Sunday, and in such case on the Monday after.

T. O., 28 *June*, 1880.

100. No departure from the usual mode of calling to the Bar be sanctioned except on motion after seven days' previous notice.

<small>Notice of departure from mode.</small>

T. O., 17 *May*, 1889.

101. It is not the custom of this Society to call to the Bar any person engaged in trade.

<small>Persons in trade.</small>

T. O., 21 *January*, 1881.

102. It is desirable that this Society should admit to the Bar such Members of the Colonial Bar who have obtained eminence and distinction thereat and may be desirous of being so admitted as the Masters of the Bench may think fit, but subject to such regulations or conditions as they may appoint.

<small>Eminent Colonial Barristers.</small>

T. O., 30 *April*, 1867.

Voluntary compounding.

103. (1) Every Barrister may at any time commute for his Annual Dues, which amount to 19*s.* 8*d.* per annum for Barristers not of the degree of Queen's Counsel, and £1 3*s.* 8*d.* for Barristers of the degree of Queen's Counsel, on the following scale:—

Between the ages of 20 and 30	...	£14
,,	,,	30 ,, 40	...	13
,,	,,	40 ,, 50	...	11
,,	,,	50 ,, 60	...	10
,,	,,	60 ,, 70	...	8

(2) Every gentleman who at the time of commutation is one of Her Majesty's Counsel shall pay £2 in addition.

(3) Every Barrister applying for a Certificate upon going abroad, shall be required, when the Certificate is granted, to compound for his Annual Dues according to the foregoing table.

(4) A receipt shall be given for the composition in the following form :—

> RECEIVED of a Barrister of the Inner Temple, the sum of £ as a composition for all future payments for Pensions and Preacher's duties to the said Society.

T. O., 23 *November*, 1869.

104. Bar dues shall not be payable by any Members of this Inn, who shall be called to the Bar after the present Term. In lieu of such Bar dues, a sum of £12 be paid to the House by each Member of the Inn on his Call to the Bar, together with other fees to the House. Compulsory compounding.

DISBARRING AND WITHDRAWING.

T. O., 21 *November*, 1879.

105. WHEN it has been proved to the Bench that a Member of this Inn has been convicted by a competent tribunal of any offence, which in Conviction of Barrister.

the opinion of the Bench disqualifies him from continuing a Member of the Inn, his name shall be removed from the books; but the Bench shall be at liberty to re-instate such person, on such cause being shewn as they shall deem satisfactory.

T. O., 11 *April*, 1878.

Becoming Solicitor.
106. A Barrister cannot enter a Solicitor's Office, or be an Articled Clerk until he has been disbarred, and if he does so, he renders himself liable to be disbarred.

T. O., 29 *May*, 1855.

Withdrawing.
107. No future application by any Barrister of this Society, not being (as a Barrister) a Member of any of the other Inns of Court, for leave to withdraw from this Society, shall be granted without a declaration signed by him that he is not practising, and that it is his intention not to practise as a Barrister in future, either in this country or in any of the colonies.

STUDENTS.

T. O., 22 *June*, 1798. (Amended 31 Jan. 1901.

108. No person who shall have been admitted or who shall hereafter be admitted (except as hereinafter excepted), into ~~any of the Inns of Court,~~ this Society shall be called to the English Bar, unless he shall, previous to his keeping any of the Terms requisite for that purpose, have deposited with the Treasurer ~~of the Society to which he belongs~~ the sum of One Hundred Pounds, the same to be returned without interest upon his being called to the Bar, or quitting the Society, or, in case of his death, to his personal representatives.

Deposit on Admission.

But this is not to excuse him from paying his duties regularly, nor from giving the usual Bond upon Admission.

Provided that this Order shall not extend to any person who shall previous to his being called to the Bar produce a Certificate of his

D

being a Member of the College of Advocates in Scotland, or of his having taken a degree or kept two years' Terms in any of the Universities of Oxford, Cambridge, Dublin, London, or Durham, or the Victoria University of Manchester, the Universities of Leeds, Liverpool, Birmingham or Wales, or the Royal University of Ireland; and in case such deposit as aforesaid shall have been made the same shall be immediately returned to him upon his producing such Certificate as is above mentioned.

T. O. 31. 1. 05.

T. O., 17 *December*, 1889.

Commons Deposit.

109. When a person is admitted into this Society, he may, if he so desire, deposit with the Treasurer the sum of £50 as security for his Commons and Dues, instead of giving the usual bond upon admission; but his giving such security shall not excuse him from making the deposit of £100 required by *T. O.*, 22 *June*, 1798 (No. 108.)

T. O., 13 *January*, 1893.

110. Students who have paid the amount of the Student's dues for four years from the date of their Admission may compound for all their future dues as Students by a present payment of £10. <small>Students compounding.</small>

Any gentleman who after compounding for his Student's dues shall be subsequently called to the Bar shall, in compounding for his Dues as a Barrister, be allowed the amount, if any, by which the £10 Composition already paid exceeds the amount of the dues which would otherwise have become payable by him as a Student.

T. O., 16 *April*, 1852.
„   27 *Oct.*, 1891.

111. No Attorney at Law, Solicitor, Writer to the Signet, or Writer of the Scotch Courts, Proctor, Notary Public, Clerk in Chancery, <small>Who may be admitted as Students.</small>

D 2

Parliamentary Agent, or Agent in any Court, original or appellate, Clerk to any Justice of the Peace, Registrar of any Court, Receiver or Liquidator, whether Official, Provisional, Assistant or Deputy, or person acting in any of these or similar capacities, and no Clerk to any such person as aforesaid, or to any Judge, Barrister, Conveyancer, Pleader, Equity Draftsman, Clerk of the Peace, or to any officer in any Court of Justice, and no person acting in the capacity of any such Clerk shall be admitted as a Student at any Inn of Court until such person shall have entirely and *bonâ fide* ceased to act or practise in any of the capacities above-named or described; and if on the Rolls of any Court, shall have taken his name off the Rolls thereof.

T. O., 3 *May,* 1889.

Privilege of Solicitors.

112. A Student who, previously to his admission at an Inn of Court, was a Solicitor in practice

for not less than five years (and, in accordance with Rule 7, has ceased to be a Solicitor before his Admission as a Student) may be examined for Call to the Bar without keeping any Terms, and may be called to the Bar upon passing the public Examination required by these Rules, without keeping any Terms;

Provided that such Solicitor has given at least twelve months' notice in writing to each of the Four Inns of Court, and to the Incorporated Law Society, of his intention to seek Call to the Bar, and produces a Certificate signed by two Members of the Council of the Incorporated Law Society that he is a fit and proper person to be called to the Bar.

A Student coming under the last preceding Rule may be exempted by the Masters of the Bench of the Inn to which he seeks Admission from passing the Examination preliminary to Admission.

54

T. O., 25 April, 1884.

Preliminary Examination.
113. In the case of a Solicitor it is unnecessary to impose a preliminary Examination, those cases being excepted where the Examination preliminary to admission as a Solicitor was dispensed with.

T. O., 4 November, 1859.

Copy of Rules.
114. In every case of admission into this Society there shall be delivered by the Sub-Treasurer to the person admitted a copy of the Rules agreed to by the Four Inns of Court.

T. O., 6 February, 1732.
„ *30 January, 1767.*

Admission gratis.
115. From henceforward none but the eldest son of a Master of the Bench be admitted *gratis* a Member of this Society as a Student.

T. O., 5 June, 1888.

Student in arrear.
116. If a Student's fees have not been paid by him for three years, a registered letter shall

In lieu of *T. O.* 116 which has been abolished, the following are substituted :—

T. O., 4 *November*, 1898.

116*a*. If a Student, who has not made a deposit on admission, shall allow his dues to become three years in arrear, a registered letter shall be sent directed to him at his last known address informing him that unless all arrears to the date of such letter be paid within six months, he will be suspended from all privileges as a Member of the Society till the further Order of the Bench; and on the expiration of such notice without payment, he shall be suspended accordingly.

116*b*. If, after a Student has been suspended under Order 116*a*, his sureties shall pay all dues incurred up to the date of the notice, they shall be entitled to be released from all further liability as sureties.

116c. No application shall be made to a Student suspended under T. O. 116a for dues incurred after his suspension, but he shall not be restored to the privileges of membership till he has paid all dues to the date of his restoration and a restoration fee of £5 and has also given a new bond with two sureties in the usual form, or has deposited with the Treasurer the sum of £50 as security for his commons and dues, and has complied with such other conditions, if any, as the Bench may impose.

be sent, directed to him at his last known address, informing him that unless all arrears be paid within six months from the date of that letter, his name will be removed from the books of the Society, but without prejudice of the claim of the Society against him and his sureties for all dues up to the date of such notice, and on the expiration of such notice his name shall be removed accordingly.

RE-ADMISSION OF STUDENTS.
J.O. 10 June 1873.

117. A STUDENT who has ceased to be a Member of the Inn may, by special permission of the Bench, be re-admitted upon his paying all dues accrued in the interval, and (unless a Member of the College of Advocates in Scotland or of the Universities of Oxford, Cambridge, Dublin, London, Durham, ~~or of~~ the Royal University of Ireland) depositing £100 *the Victoria University of Manchester, the Universities of Leeds, Liverpool, Birmingham or Wales, or J.O. 31 1.05* {Conditions of re-admission.}

and producing a Certificate in the usual form satisfactory to the Treasurer.

T. O., 13 *November*, 1832.

Former terms and standing allowed.

118. Gentlemen having deposited £100, with a view of being called to the Bar in England, and subsequently quitting the Society, shall be allowed in the event of re-admission and re-deposit of the £100 to have, for the purpose of being called to the Bar, the advantage of the former Terms kept, and of a standing equal to the time between the first admission and the quitting the Society, provided that the claim for re-admission shall in such cases be laid before the Bench.

COMMONS AND DUES.

T. O., 7 *July*, 1704.

Duration.

119. The Term Commons shall not commence before the first day of the Term, nor

continue longer than the last, except to end half a week.

T. O., 4 February, 1734.

120. No Commons are allowed to be served to any Bencher in the Parliament Chamber, nor any gowns hung there. — Parliament Chamber not to be used.

T. O., 23 April, 1861.

121. The charge to the Benchers for dinners shall be 3s., and each Bencher shall be charged for seven dinners for each Term, in each case whether present or not, and payment at the rate of 3s. per diem. shall be made by all Benchers who may dine beyond the prescribed number. — Benchers' charge for Dinner.

122. No alteration to be made in the Regulation by which nothing is paid by the Benchers for dinners on the adjournment days out of Term. — Dinners out of Term.

T. O., 25 May, 1875.

Barristers' charge.

123. All Barristers shall pay ready money for their dinners, at the present rate of 3*s.* per dinner.

T. O., 5 April, 1867.

Students' charge.

124. The charge for Students' dinners shall be one guinea for the Term, and 3*s.* 6*d.* a day for every day a Student dines beyond the number of six.

T. O., 6 February, 1778.

Vacations &c. abolished.

125. After this present Hilary Term vacations and amerciaments to be abolished, and every Student to pay in lieu thereof the sum of £5 before he enters into Commons, and every gentleman called to the Bar to pay £10 as a composition in lieu of vacations and amerciaments after his Call to the Bar.

59

T. O., 27 June, 1876.

126. It is an instruction to the Treasurer or Acting Treasurer not to give permission to any Student to leave the Hall before 7 o'clock unless grace after dinner shall be sooner said.

Students leaving Hall.

T. O., 27 June, 1876.

127. Newspapers shall not be read in Hall during the hour of dinner, and a copy of this Order shall be screened in the Hall.

Newspapers in Hall.

T. O., 9 November, 1729.

128. No Barrister to come into Commons without his Bar gown.

Gowns.

T. O., 20 November, 1821.

129. No Student hereafter admitted to Commons, shall be allowed to dine in Commons more than twenty Terms, except in the Term in which he shall apply to be Called to the Bar.

Not more than twenty Terms to be kept.

T. O., 5 February, 1819.

Table of Fees. 130. A Table of Fees payable for Admissions, Commons and Chambers, on Calls to the Bar, and on Certificates to be placed in the Hall.

T. O., 13 February, 1827.

Entry of names. 131. Names of all gentlemen dining in the Hall to be taken in writing daily.

T. O., 27 January, 1824.

Accounts. 132. The Collector is directed to deliver an account half-yearly after Hilary and Trinity Terms, of all sums owing for Dues, Commons, Pensions, Preacher's Duties and Gowns to every Bencher, Barrister and Student.

T. O., 2 June, 1725.

Pensions and Preacher's duties. 133. The Members of this Society shall discharge the Pensions and Preacher's Duties yearly.

T. O., 4 *November*, 1884.

134. An account of all gentlemen in arrear to be laid before the Masters of the Bench, on the 15th May and 15th November in every year, and before the Auditors. — Arrears.

CHURCH.

T. O., 29 *October*, 1691.
„ 22 *November*, 1741.
„ 10 *June*, 1771.

135. THE appointment of an Afternoon Preacher to the Temple Church and of a Preacher on Fast Days is vested alternately (each sermon) in the two Societies. The Clergyman's fee on such occasion is £2 2s. — Afternoon Preacher.

T. O., 4 *May*, 1841.

136. The Treasurer, and failing him any Bencher, has the appointment for any vacant Sundays. — Appointment.

T. O., 6 *February*, 1783.

<small>Preacher not appearing.</small> 137. In case the Afternoon Preacher shall not appear in the Preacher's seat at the church before the prayers are ended, the Reader is to preach and receive the gratuity.

T. O., 30 *January*, 1792.

<small>Preacher's Deputy.</small> 138. If the Clergyman appointed to preach the Afternoon Sermon shall not attend in person, but send a proper person to preach, such Deputy may perform the duty, but the fee is not to be paid until the Treasurer shall give an order to that effect; and if the Clergyman deputed shall decline preaching, the Reader is to supply his place and receive the stipend.

T. O., 6 *November*, 1883.

<small>Church Orders.</small> 139. Masters of the Bench, not being Honorary Members thereof, are entitled to give orders for three persons to the Morning Service; but

there is no restriction in respect of the Afternoon Service.

Owing to the limited accommodation of the Benchers' stalls, orders are not given to admit to them; but any Bencher can bring a friend with him to the supplementary seats.

T. O., 13 *June*, 1862.

140. Any Bencher or Barrister of the Inn may introduce two ladies. — Introducing ladies.

T. O., 24 *May*, 1816.

141. No monument or tablet to be placed in the Body or Round of the Church until the plan, size and place be first approved of by two of the Masters of the Bench. — Monuments.

T. O., 27 *January*, 1843.

142. No sum of money shall be laid out on the Church without Special Order of the Bench. — Expenditure on Church.

T. O., 2 May, 1851.

No money to Church Servants.

143. No money shall be given to the servants of the Church, and any servant receiving any fee or gratuity from any visitor shall be immediately discharged.

T. O., 13 June, 1862.

No fee for admission.

144. No servant in the Church is permitted to receive money for the admission of a stranger.

SUB-TREASURER.

T. O., 6 February, 1821.

Forms.

145. The following forms to be printed for the use of the Sub-Treasurer, *viz.:*—

    Chamber, Bar, Commons Bonds.
    Composition and Deposit Papers.
    Certificates for Admission into Commons.
    Letters for Payment of Pensions and Preacher's Duties.

T. O., 26 June, 1821.

146. The Sub-Treasurer's Clerk to be employed in continuing an Index to the Bench Table Orders. *Index.*

T. O., 15 June, 1695.

147. Sub-Treasurer to deliver a particular alphabetically of all bonds in his custody to every new Treasurer on his admission. *Bonds.*

T. O., 13 November, 1780.

148. It is the duty of the Sub-Treasurer to inspect the conduct of the several servants of the House, and report to the Table if he finds any of them deficient in their duty. *Control of servants.*

Addition to T. O. 145.
T. O., 21 November, 1880.

149. If any servant of the House be guilty of serious misconduct in his office, the Treasurer or in his absence the Sub-Treasurer, *Misconduct by Servants.*

shall have power to suspend him; but if this shall happen within four days before any business day of the Bench, the same shall be reported to the Bench, and if it shall happen at any other time, it shall be reported to the Treasurer, who shall have power, on investigation, to remove or continue the suspension or dismiss the servant.

T. O., 25 *November,* 1757.

Book of Commons.

150. The account of Commons, Pensions, and Preacher's Duties shall be entered in a book or books to be kept for that purpose.

T. O., 5 *November,* 1682.

Attendance of Sub-Treasurer.

151. Sub-Treasurer to attend at every Parliament and enter Acts, &c.

T. O., 9 *May,* 1692.

Members' Names taken down.

152. Sub-Treasurer to put down in a book kept for the entry of Bench Orders the

names of all Benchers present at the making of any Bench Table Order, and if any Bencher then present shall dissent to any Order then proposed to be made, every such Bencher shall and may at the time be at liberty to enter his dissent or protestation thereunto.

T. O., 29 *April*, 1884.

153. Any person in the employment of the Inn who shall make any unauthorised communication respecting the business of the Inn to the Papers, shall be subject to be punished and dismissed. Communication to Papers

HOUSE.

T. O., 26 *November*, 1819.

154 INVENTORIES of all things belonging to the Society given in charge to the Officers of the House shall in future be delivered to each Treasurer upon his coming into office. Inventories.

T. O., 21 *February*, 1851.

Newspapers in Parliament Chamber.

155. No person whatever shall under any circumstances take from the Parliament Chamber any of the daily newspapers, reviews, magazines or other periodicals; except that the Master of the Temple shall, as heretofore, be permitted to take the daily newspapers in the evenings, out of Term only, to be returned by him before 12 o'clock on the following day to the Treasurer's Office, where they are to be kept filed, and no person whatever shall take from the Parliament Chamber any of the Sunday papers until their places have been supplied by the succeeding number.

T. O. 18 *February*, 1835.

Notice as to papers to be screened.

156. A notice shall be affixed in the Parliament Chamber requesting that the reviews, magazines, newspapers, periodicals and publications may not be removed in future until such time as their places have been respectively

supplied by the succeeding numbers or number of the work.

T. O. 31 *October*, 1702.

157. Clean linen to be prepared for all the tables in the Hall every day. {Clean Linen.}

T. O. 12 *June*, 1860.

158. No person eligible to be a waiter in the Hall, unless he shall have been for two years employed as a servant in a family, or as a waiter. {Waiters.}

ACCOUNTS.

T. O., 19 *January*, 1883.

159. In the accounts of the Inn presented to the Bench every six months, at the Audit Dinner, the item " General Repairs," shall be divided into at least two separate heads, *e.g.*— {Repairs to be separately entered.}

  1.—Ordinary Repairs.
  2.—Permanent Repairs.

so as to shew clearly on the face of the accounts how large a per centage on rental is expended in ordinary wear and tear, and how much on exceptional objects of a different description.

T. O., 13 *November,* 1753.

Sale of Stock.

160. No stock purchased or to be purchased shall be disposed of but in pursuance of an Order of the Bench Table, to be made on a particular day appointed for that purpose, and notice of such day shall be given at least three days before to all the Masters of the Bench then in Town.

SURVEYOR, &c.

T. O., 10 *June,* 1777.

Orders for Work.

161. In future no work to be done by any workman without an order from Treasurer, Sub-Treasurer or Surveyor, and the workmen

shall specify in their bills by whose order and where such work was done.

T. O., 9 *November*, 1819.

162. No tradesman shall begin any work until he receive instructions from the Surveyor, except any trifling repairs which may be ordered by the Sub-Treasurer, the vouchers for which to be delivered by the tradesman to the Surveyor as often as required, that the necessary examination may be made at the time when the work is done.

Instructions to Workmen.

T. O., 19 *January*, 1883.

163. No structural alteration in the external features of any building in the Inner Temple, and no alteration in the external colouring of any building, gate or railing in the Inner Temple shall be made without a written authority from the Bench previously obtained by the Surveyor,

Authority for Structural Alteration.

but in cases of sudden emergency the written sanction of the Treasurer shall be a sufficient authority.

GENERAL.

Saving Order. 164. Nothing herein contained shall affect the validity of any Act of Parliament or Table Order not mentioned herein.

www.ingramcontent.com/pod-product-compliance
Lightning Source LLC
Chambersburg PA
CBHW032249080426
42735CB00008B/1070